Pattern Sourcebook:
Around the World
250 Patterns for Projects and Designs

Shigeki Nakamura

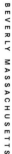

BEVERLY MASSACHUSETTS

ROCKPORT PUBLISHERS

First published in the United States of America by
Rockport Publishers, a member of
Quayside Publishing Group
100 Cummings Center
Suite 406-L
Beverly, Massachusetts 01915-6101
Telephone: (978) 282-9590
Fax: (978) 283-2742
www.rockpub.com

ISBN-13: 978-1-59253-496-8
ISBN-10: 1-59253-496-1

10 9 8 7 6 5 4 3 2

Printed in Singapore

Preface

Although ethnic groups each have their own structure and characteristics, they also possess something we may call "an original form." Despite the fact that people throughout the world have the unprecedented opportunity for cultural interchange, the original form of a culture may not change. So, the difficulty that comes with sharing the sense of aesthetics may lie in the challenge of trying to look inside the ethnic spirit that has not been lost. For the Japanese people this may be even more difficult because Japan does not share its borders with any other country.

However, it may be simpler than we think if we just enjoy comparing the pure structures in the designs created, nurtured, and disseminated by an ethnic group. Consider when people are asked to associate a word with "Japanese image," they may answer, "Mount Fuji" or "cherry blossoms." And when asked about an "American image," they may answer "horse-drawn wagons," or "stars." These easily understood images and symbols are powerful factors in convincing others of the sharing of aesthetics.

In addition, what is even more important is to understand images at a much deeper level. Even in the same realm of Islam, for instance, expressions of the same motif are different, and the desires of a particular ethnic group are at the base of their emotional attachment. The aim of this book is to find a way for even Japan to share in the sense of aesthetics by clarifying a little the background to the conditions that have made a country what it is and how that is expressed in art forms.

The book has been structured without categorizing the traditional designs according to their historical art forms. Instead, we have divided the book into five geographical areas and analyzed each separately.

The actual patterns that form the groundwork for the book have not been incorporated just as they are. We have included many patterns that have been originally developed and then modified in order to make their appeal more accessible. The depth and maturity of the historical color tones used in designs on cloth, buildings, or other materials could be viewed as one decisive factor in expressing the national characteristics of a country. However, please note that we have slightly adapted color tones for easier comprehension.

By looking at the patterns in this book and on the CD-ROM, we believe that you should be able to easily uncover the themes that you want to develop in your designs. We hope that you will find endless ways to use this book to assist you for your work or hobbies.

Shigeki Nakamura (Cobble Collaboration)

Contents

How to use this book

All of the designs introduced in this book are included on the CD-ROM. Please use the materials after reading this page and page 160 of this book.

Explanatory note

● Materials in the designs have been extracted from the existing traditional designs in order to focus on the main points specified in the text of this book.

● Our main aim is to present the patterns in a way that the structure of the design can be used for development. Consequently, we have modified many of the designs to present them with our own original layout and coloring. Although the designs are based on the traditional designs from specific countries or on the special patterns from certain periods, they are not the designs in their original forms.

● The files, on the CD-ROM are, in principle, complete unit samples, but the images used in the book have been trimmed to fit the layout in some cases the colors have been partially modified.

Page Layout

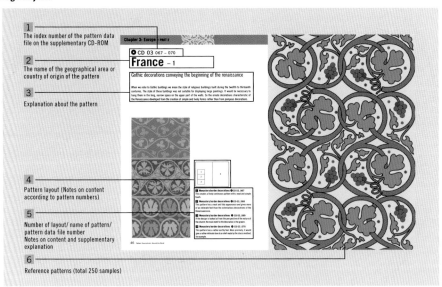

1
The index number of the pattern data file on the supplementary CD-ROM

2
The name of the geographical area or country of origin of the pattern

3
Explanation about the pattern

4
Pattern layout (Notes on content according to pattern numbers)

5
Number of layout/ name of pattern/ pattern data file number
Notes on content and supplementary explanation

6
Reference patterns (total 250 samples)

Chapter 1
Asia

● CD 01 001 – 004

Japan – 1

The aesthetic feelings and view of the world held by the culturally unique Japanese

Although the Japanese import civilization and culture from all over the world, they mercilessly dismiss anything that does not suit them. Also, the parts that are integrated into the culture are adapted and perfected in a particularly Japanese way.

	4
1	
2	
3	

1 Fan pattern ● CD 01_001

The special shapes and patterns of fans form part of the summer tradition in Japan, naturally expressing Japanese aesthetic beauty.

2 Lines of brushes ● CD 01_002

Objects that are used in our everyday lives are extravagantly beautified.

3 Pine needles and cherry blossoms ● CD 01_003

This is an original design without a deep contrast that conveys a relaxed sense of nature inclining towards sophistication.

4 Japanese pampas grass ● CD 01_004

The way that all aspects of human nature are reflected in this

● CD 01 005 – 008

Japan – 2

Giving priority to expressing the feel of the motif rather than the original form

In the many artistic figures originating from Buddhism manji, or the Buddhist Cross is the most representative pattern among the symbols used at Buddhist temples. Originally, there were both dextral (going to the right) and sinistral (going to the left) designs but Japan completely ignored the form and just chose one design that would make a beautiful pattern for kimono and rejected the rest. The archetypal pattern of the Buddhist Cross is broken down to form variations in the design.

1	4
2	
3	

1 Connecting in flux ● CD 01_005
The rotational feel to the circular image of the design is more concretely emphasized in this design.

2 The cross and diagonal shapes ● CD 01_006
Rather than presenting a three-dimensional image of the cross, this original design aims to transform the three-dimensional shape.

3 Disconnected shapes ● CD 01_007
This is an extremely imaginative transformation of the cross into a flamboyant design. The composition of the pattern has the feel of simplified beauty and heightened perfection.

4 Peony arabesque design of Hitatare ● CD 01_008
Priests and people of high social standing used special regal patterns for clothing and furniture, but it was also considered appropriate for samurai to wear such patterns to provide a sense of beauty when they committed ritual suicide.

■ **Orchid pattern on Nabeshima dish** ● CD 01_009 Even for small things in nature the traditional Japanese sense is to preserve the elegance whilst creating a design of magnanimous quality.

■ **Big Wave by Kohrin** ● CD 01_010   The perfect beauty of this composition led to the pattern taking the name of the designer (Kohrin). The pattern is a representative craft design that is both sensitive and dynamic, reflecting the view of life and death held by the Japanese people.

● CD 01 011 – 014

China – 1

The diverse identity of China: A powerful country of many ethnic groups

The ancient designs used in Japan were strongly influenced by Chinese decorations.

1	
2	4
3	

1 2 3 Wooden temple decorations
● CD 01_011, 012, 013
A representative arabesque pattern that strongly conveys a Buddhist atmosphere.

4 Design interpreting earthquakes
● CD 01_014
This is an elaborate pattern that illustrates the folklore belief that when an earthquake occurs the decorative dragons release copper balls from their mouths.

■ **Wooden decoration on a pavilion** ● CD 01_015 Expression of the combination of two types of arabesque designs used, for example, on pavilion roofs.

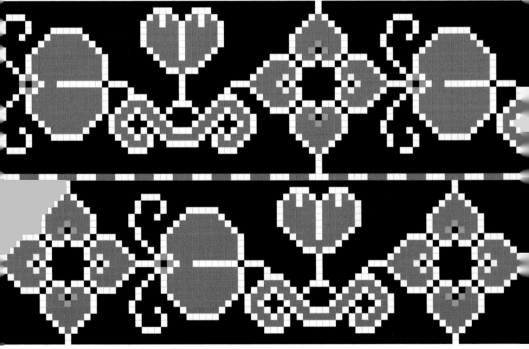

■ **Miao dynasty belt** ● CD 01_016 A beautifully embroidered colorful pattern for the belts that members of the Miao ethnic minority group traditionally wear on their hips. The Miao people often use peach blossoms in their designs.

■ **Latticework on a building** ● CD 01_017   A latticework pattern used for windows and partitions. A dignified design that is said to be the original form of the interlocking circular pattern of Japan's "symbol of the seven treasures."

■ **Wooden decoration for a pavilion** ● CD 01_018   There appears to be the abstract impression of a dragon which is a conventional image for pavilion decorations. However, even historical evidence has not been able to fully establish the background to this pattern.

● **CD 01** 019 – 021

China – 2

Chinese floral latticework designs

In China it could almost be said that each artifact has a different lattice pattern, otherwise known as "hanakoushi" or floral latticework. An abundant supply of latticework materials still remain and all of them are very beautiful and befitting of the name "floral latticework." Among them are some magnificent designs which we rarely have the chance to see. The designs have a surprisingly large number of variations as well.

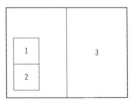

1 2 Latticework building decoration
● CD 01_019, 20
Historical evidence cannot be found to ascertain the buildings or parts of buildings for which these designs were used. However, it is surprising to see the large number of variations of the same style.

3 Border designs on buildings ● CD 01_021
This takes the same form as a design on the borders of one of the three famous Chinese stone caves (Dunhuang caves). Again, this is an original Chinese pattern illustrating the myriad variations of an identical form.

■ **Latticework building decoration** ○ **CD 01_022, 023, 024, 025** Just as in sample numbers 19 and 20, it is fascinating to see the way that the style of these designs has evolved. Historical evidence cannot be found to ascertain the buildings or parts of buildings for which these designs were used but the identical style and wide variation of designs are impressive.

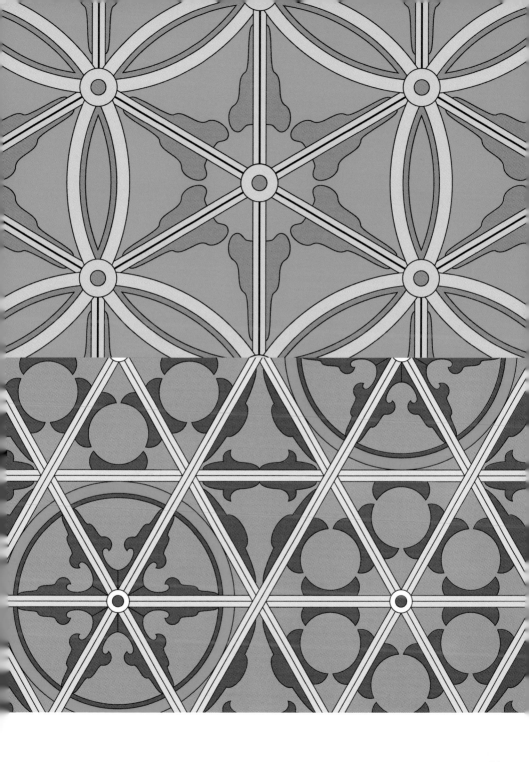

● CD 01 026 – 029

South Korea

Patterns that combine flamboyancy with a restrained and quiet beauty

Having being ruled by Imperial China, the Korean people were deeply influenced by Confucianism. This profound influence from China can be seen in the patterns of the designs as well. However, one aspect that is different to the flawless composure of the Chinese style designs is the way that the Korean patterns combine a particularly restrained beauty in the extremely colorful effect of their designs. Above all, when used as temple decorations these flamboyant designs convey the reverse side to the sense of transience.

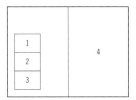

1 Korean Chrysanthemum pattern ● CD 01_026
The Japanese chrysanthemum pattern has a solid or realistic shape that looks as if it could be mathematically divided. In comparison, the Korean chrysanthemum pattern lies more towards the middle of the range of softness.

2 Embroidered cloth ● CD 01_027
This pattern is based on the Buddhist cross symbol that is often used in Korea. Some parts are identical to the Chinese latticework patterns but the Korean designs tend to convey more of a bright and colorful ornamental feel.

3 An arrangement of embroidered patterns
● CD 01_028
This design is reminiscent of the Japanese furoshiki (wrapping cloth). The special features bring the material to life.

4 An arrangement of embroidered patterns
● CD 01_29
In the midst of this flamboyant design there is a blend of a sense of intimacy and sweetness. Such decorative work is often seen on everyday items in Korea.

⊙ CD 01 030 – 033

Vietnan and Indonesia

A sense of nostalgia, an emotion shared by all ethnic groups

Since long ago, materials such as the well-known calico fabric of Java have been associated with Indonesia. The calico patterns, wherever they are made, make Japanese people feel nostalgic. The common trait shared by all Asian cultures is that they can accept the figures in the patterns, whatever they are, without any feeling of discomfort. This is because the designs that have been introduced into their daily lives express the sense of closeness to nature that people feel.

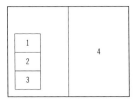

1 Balinese batik ⊙ CD 01_030
Traditional Indonesian cloth (batik) fabric is used for some of the local customary dress. When bright colors are used boldly it has a tropical feel to it.

2 Javanese calico ⊙ CD 01_031
This is a rather unique Javanese calico pattern. With its refined appearance it looks suitable for ceremonial occasions whilst also emanating an amiable beauty.

3 Vietnamese tapestry ⊙ CD01_032
A solid and dignified design made by using natural plant dyes.

4 A sarong (Indonesian cloth for wrapping around the waist) ⊙ CD 01_033
The rough feel of the way the pattern appears to be quickly stuck

⊙ CD 01 034 – 036

Tibet and Nepal

The ethnic feeling of Tibet and Nepal is boldly revealed

Tibet and Nepal cannot be viewed as the same country. However, the strong influence of India and Britain on Nepal, and China on Tibet, is noticeable. It may be difficult to judge from the examples of patterns shown here, but it is very interesting that a solid ethnic identity can be perceived even when we view the colors from a religious perspective (Hindu or Buddhist).

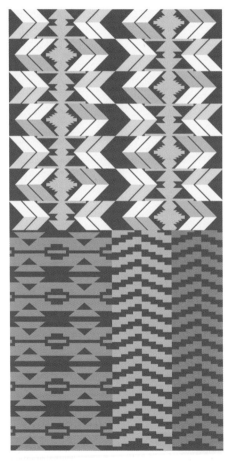

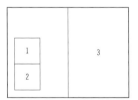

1 Nepalese weaving ⊙ CD 01_034
The pattern in the cloth is woven in the same way on the reverse side and is used in Nepal as a belt as well.

2 Nepalese weaving ⊙ CD 01_035
Quiet and calm pattern and coloring. It seems to express the image of the shape of the mountains that the Nepalese view every day.

3 Tibetan Cloth ⊙ CD 01_036
Although one aspect of this design is its strong representation of Buddhism, the structure of the pattern is difficult for Japanese

CD 01 037 – 039

India

A vivid image of India expressed in the colors and patterns

It is said that the Indian people can tell at a glance which caste people belong to. As Japanese we do not know whether this judgment is made according to clothing or language. However even without concrete figures such as elephants and dolls, the "image of India" is expressed by the formation of the patterns and the use of colors.

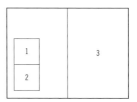

1	3
2	

1 Indigo cloth dyed by the woodblock method
 CD 01_037
The appearance is similar to cloth dyed by the Japanese indigo dyeing (Aizome) method but the clear difference in the pattern lies in the simplicity of the method used.

2 Jacquard wrapping cloth CD 01_038
This kind of pattern is generally accepted as being the most representative of India.

3 A plant-dyed fabric pattern CD 01_039
As in sample number 38, this design also has a special pattern that conveys the atmosphere of Indian charm.

■ **Indian cotton cloth** ● CD 01_040 This lovely pattern is a simplified reproduction of paisley, a pattern that expresses the vitality of plant life. It is a multi-use pattern that can change the atmosphere whichever way it is used.

Chapter 2
Europe – 1
Germany

● CD 02 041 – 044
Germany – 1

Traditional pattern designs in each area of Europe and the shared sense of aesthetics

The Germanic people had already almost created the original form of modern Germany as far back as the middle ages (eighth century). Although it is true that in many ways they retained the legacy left by the Roman Empire. After the passage of some time it is thought that the German people developed a refined artistic sensitivity through their production of many figures of high cultural standing and the collection of works of art by the famous Hapsburg family.

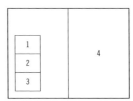

1 2 3 4 Floral patterns on fabric from the middle ages ● CD 02_041, 042, 043, 044
The simplified and realistic depictions of flowers in the patterns are often used even now as reference material.

● CD 02 045 – 048
Germany – 2

The high cultural level in Europe conveyed by the floral patterns of the Middle Ages

The floral designs shown here have been selected from the collection of Kamei Koreaki who spent a year studying in Germany (1886). As both the period and country of production are completely unknown, we have put them in the German section. This beautiful group of patterns offers us a glimpse of the high level of cultural refinement throughout Europe.

1	4
2	
3	

1 2 3 4 Floral patterns on fabric
from the Middle Ages ● CD 02_045, 046, 047, 048
This group of patterns strongly conveys the sense of artistic design.

■ **Floral patterns on fabric from the Middle Ages** ◉ CD 02_049, 050, 051, 052 These designs have fairly large floral patterns. These patterns could also be used for modern wallpaper.

■ **Continuous patterns on fabric from the Middle Ages** ◉ CD 02_053, 054, 055, 056 A relatively elevated sense of design is required to express the motif in a continuous pattern.

■ **Border decorations on fabric from the Middle Ages** ◉ CD 02_057, 058, 059, 060 These patterns have a healthy brightness to them and look like they would add a touch of enjoyment to daily life.

⊙ CD 02 061 – 064

Germany – 3

Germany during the Renaissance: a slight departure from classical Europe

The patterns produced in Germany during the Renaissance period are a little different than the bright and glittering ones generated by the artistic movement of the Italian Renaissance (1400–1600 A.D.) Art that was protected and preserved by the royalty or the church also bore some relation to the German Protestant Reformation. However, we do not know the extent to which that influenced the artists.

1	
2	4
3	

1 2 3 Building border decorations during the Renaissance ⊙ CD 02_061, 062, 063

Although many of these patterns are rather elaborate, they also emanate a simple, flowing beauty.

4 Cupboard decoration with wooden inlay ⊙ CD 02_064

This is a dignified, symmetrical pattern that is not over-

■ **Wall decorations on buildings** ◉ CD 02_065   This design has a rather precise and heavy warmth to it.

■ **Tile pattern** ◉ CD 02_066   This pattern reminds us of the pomegranate tree designs often seen in countries such as Greece. The balance of the leaves in the design is beautiful.

Chapter 3
Europe – 2
France

● CD 03 067 – 070
France – 1

Gothic decorations conveying the beginning of the renaissance

When we refer to Gothic buildings we mean the style of religious buildings built during the twelfth to thirteenth centuries. The style of these buildings was not suitable for displaying large paintings. It would be necessary to hang them in the long, narrow space on the upper part of the walls. So the ornate decorations characteristic of the Renaissance developed from the creation of simple and lively forms rather than from pompous decorations.

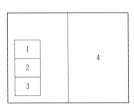

1 Monastery border decorations ● CD 03_067
This creates a lively continuous pattern with a neat and simple touch.

2 Monastery border decorations ● CD 03_068
This pattern has a neat and tidy appearance and gives more of an intimate feel than the ostentatious decorations of the Renaissance era.

3 Monastery border decorations ● CD 03_069
If the design is looked at from the perspective of the nature of the church, the main motif in the decoration is the grapes.

4 Monastery border decorations ● CD 03_070
This pattern has a rather earthy feel. More precisely, it would give a rather intimate tone to a relief made by the stucco method, for example.

● CD 03 071 – 074
France – 2

Printing technology led to the development of elegant decorations created by the simplification of design reproduction

Renaissance is a French word meaning "rebirth." Although the Renaissance culture mainly flourished in Italy, the concept probably took root in France. The development of printing technology that took place in France simplified the elaborate methods of reproducing designs and created an aesthetic realm not emulated in Italy.

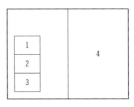

1 **A wall design produced by stucco workmanship**
● CD 03_071
This is a design that does not give an impression of antiquity and is widely used even now.

2 **Tapestry border decoration** ● CD 03_072
Dull colors were popular during this era. This design, however, is enhanced by the use of bright tones.

3 **Part of a book page design** ● CD 03_073
This decorative design is in wide use. The form of the pattern is used throughout the world even now.

4 **Part of an embroidered pattern** ● CD 03_074
Such comprehensive patterns that are easy to develop were comparatively widespread in the period before the Renaissance.

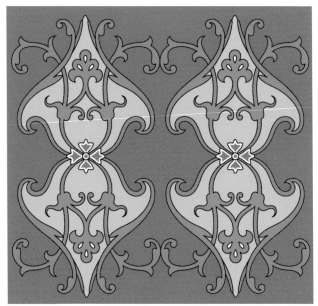

■ **Part of a tapestry** ● CD 03_075 When the shapes in the design are lined up they show a unique movement. Even looking at it now, this design has a sense of freshness.

■ **Part of a book page design** ● CD 03_076 As the three parts of this design have all been made separately, they can be used independently.

■ **Tapestry** ● **CD 03_077** This is one way that the design number "75" was developed during the Renaissance.

■ **Part of an embroidered pattern** ● CD 03_078 Patterns in the latter part of the Renaissance tended to be extravagantly over-decorative but ones like this belong to a category of patterns that are most easy to use.

■ **Border decoration on pottery** ● CD 03_079 The beauty of this design is created by the balance between the thick and thin lines.

■ **Bookbinding** ● **CD 03_080** A reproduction of a border pattern from the Renaissance period. This elaborate representation is superb.

■ **Four examples of marble church floor designs** ◉ CD 03_081, 082, 083, 084   The artistic style that followed the Renaissance is known as baroque. During this period the demand for marbling grew at an astounding rate. The people of that time must have been in awe of the majestic atmosphere in their churches created by the geometric patterns in the designs.

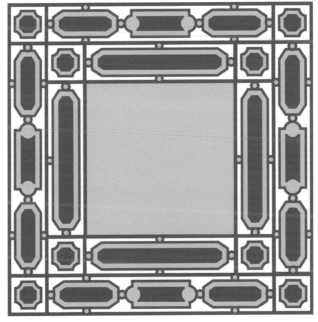

■ **Stained glass border decoration** ● CD 03_085

■ **Stained glass border decoration** ● CD 03_086   This is a pattern that originated in the time before Christ. It was a popular pattern representing the holy acanthus plant. The difference between this pattern and that of the Japanese honeysuckle (*Lanicera Japonica*) is that this design was skillfully developed at the same time as pictures on stained glass windows.

Chapter 4
Europe – 3
Italy, Greece

● CD 04 087 – 089
Italy – 1

Impressive designs that are beautifully displayed convey a powerful image

Italy has a long history of over 3,000 years. The Roman Empire that took over from the Greek civilization left a major cultural imprint. The designs that remain in the ruins from the civilization in an era before Christ have a universal appeal. In summary, the main focus was to "beautifully decorate" and with that aim they excelled in producing materials with strong aesthetic qualities. The designs that were created in this geographical area have left their spirituality and magic to posterity.

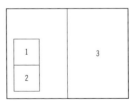

1 Border designs on ancient buildings
● CD 04_087
This is the earliest period when the acanthus pattern was used. And although the shapes are clear and simple, it produces a superior overall effect.

2 Border designs on ancient buildings
● CD 04_088
The spiral pattern gives a lively impression. It appears to be a design that can be developed in many different ways.

3 Border designs on ancient buildings
● CD 04_089
This continuous arabesque pattern has the most well-balanced design. There is an elementary feel to the composition of the elements in the design.

⦿ CD 04 090 – 092
Italy – 2

Designs from an ancient civilization that retain a universal aesthetic appeal

Art in the Roman Byzantine era (around 300-600 A.D.) is called the Byzantine style. As the area that was ruled by Rome was so vast, little difference can be perceived between these designs and those from the Mediterranean area. This is mainly due to the influence on the artisans of the high level of aesthetic appreciation established by the ancient Greek civilization.

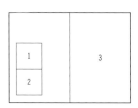

1 Border designs on ancient buildings
⦿ CD 04_090
Patterns that were painted in long and narrow spaces can be transformed in many ways depending on how they are combined.

2 Border designs on ancient buildings
⦿ CD 04_091
This design has a different atmosphere about it. When it is used as a border pattern it can be adapted as a tasteful corner decoration.

3 Border designs on ancient buildings
⦿ CD 04_092
Like sample number 90, this design also has great potential to be varied.

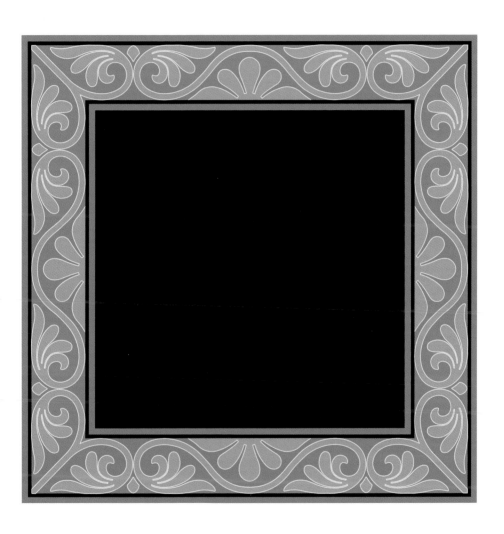

■ **Byzantine-style mosaic** ● CD 04_093, 094, 095   The way that these simple shapes are fitted together can represent an expression of infinity.

■ **Byzantine-style mosaic** ◉ **CD 04_096, 097, 098, 099** The precise lines are arranged to form a crystal-like design. These examples show the regal construction of the geometric designs.

● CD 04 100 – 103
Italy –3

A wide variety of shapes and colors forming solid designs that can easily be arranged and used today

Stained glass windows are more common in Gothic buildings than in Romanesque buildings. Although stained glass has quite a religious association, the flamboyancy and variety of shapes in these patterns result in an appealing appearance to the detailed parts of the decorations. We are in awe of such universal designs that can be arranged and used even today.

	3
1	
2	4

1 2 3 4 Wooden inlay for the interior of a church
● CD 04_100, 101, 102, 103
These detailed geometric patterns made from wood differ from the wall paintings of this period in that they portray the transformation of a powerful image by the use of color.

● CD 04 104 – 107
Italy – 4

The zenith of the Renaissance period characterized by flamboyant and decorative patterns.

This lively era produced outstanding artists such as Botticelli, Di Vinci and Michelangelo, one after another like shining stars. The designs as well demonstrate the unrestricted change from the ancient style. In all kinds of crafts as well we can see a decorativeness that could be considered excessive. One reason for this was that the decorations made for buildings moved away from laborious statues and toward diverse, bright colors.

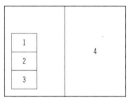

1 Part of the decoration on the capital of a temple column ● CD 04_104
It is interesting to notice that the splashing dolphin figures in the patterns are similar to the shachihoko (dolphinlike fish used in Japanese decorations.)

2 Part of a wall decoration ● CD 04_105
There are many patterns representing plants, such as the acanthus, but this design strikes the observer as a little unusual. The pattern has been developed to give more meaning to the design.

3 Part of a fish-market wall decoration ● CD 04_106
This pattern can convey a feeling of antiquity depending on how it is used. But you never grow tired of looking at the well-made arabesque design.

4 Part of a tombstone decoration ● CD 04_107
Although this pattern is used on tombstones, the beautiful design can also be used in many other ways as well.

■ **Decoration on a column of a building** ◗ CD 04_108 This pattern has a detailed and elegant design and reminds us of a salon in the rococo era. It is a pattern that seems to suggest the noble atmosphere of that era.

■ **Church bracketing** ◗ CD 04_109 It is difficult to tell the original shape from this adaptation, but the dainty flowers within the thick ukegi (vortex) are superb.

■ **Pattern on the back of playing cards** ● CD 04_110   This streamline pattern, which incorporates animal forms like hidden pictures, is magnificent.

■ **Pattern on the back of playing cards** ● CD 04_111   The arrangement of the animals, nature's messengers, in this arabesque design gives it an exotic appeal.

● CD 04 112 – 115
Greece

Designs expressing majestic beauty and the life force of the natural world

Greece is often described as the area where the foundations of western culture originated, and we can see the original shapes in parts of these patterns that were later adapted and transformed. The Chinese zigzag motif, also used in Japan and other countries, evolved from the Greek decorative designs. They used materials that have a strong life force to create these designs that are considered majestic, noble, and graceful, rather than religious.

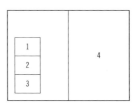

1 Decoration on the capital of a temple column
● CD 04_112
This is an excellent continuous pattern that results in a three-dimensional effect. It incorporates a design that provides a clear finish to the pattern.

2 Decoration on the capital of a temple column
● CD 04_113
This is an adaptation of the acanthus pattern that appeared from ancient times (Assyria, around 2,000 BC.)

3 Decoration on the capital of a temple column
● CD 04_114
A combination of palm and acanthus patterns.

4 Temple roof-tile ● CD 04_115
This pattern is the same as in sample number 114. It is a compactly organized pattern that conveys a majestic atmosphere.

■ **Terra-cotta pattern** ● **CD 04_116, 117** It was popular to use this kind of pattern for all kinds of designs, from temples to pottery.

■ **Decoration on the capital of a temple column** ● CD 04_118 There are some elements in this design that are hard to use but the precisely measured image of the design creates an exotic feel.

■ **Terra-cotta pattern** ● **CD 04_119** This ingenious and successful adaptation of the palm and acanthus pattern produces a striking effect. I hope that many people will use this kind of technique as a reference.

Chapter 5
Europe – 4
England, Switzerland, Holland, Austria

● CD 05 120 – 123
England – 1

The subtleness of English decorations

Many of the designs that we have come to simply call the "English style" are traditional decorative patterns that originated in the Gothic era (1200-1400 A.D.) The dignified crests used by the royal family are extremely old. Shields from Edward II's reign (around 1300 A.D.), with the three lion heads lined up in a vertical row, still remain. And although these decorations were used in the same Renaissance era, they convey a sense of refined elegance.

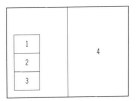

1 Tudor rose design ● CD 05_120
A pattern of overlapping white and red roses is known as "Tudor Rose." Although it is now used in all kinds of crafts, this design was originally used as a decoration for Gothic buildings.

2 Church arch decoration ● CD 05_121
This was quite a plain design for the latter part of the Renaissance. We can see evidence of the Anglo-Saxon penchant to resist imitation in such designs.

3 Ceiling decoration ● CD 05_122
This is similar to design number 121. It seems to have a completely different shape when various devices are used in the coloring to reverse the strong and weak colors.

4 Gothic building decoration ● CD 05_123
This is a Westminster arabesque pattern. The elements of the traditional design have been modified but the dignity of the design has not been lost at all.

● CD 05   124 – 126
England – 2

Victorian style—a refined beauty that does not go as far as gaudiness

The period when England most flourished was the Victorian era (the reign of Queen Victoria, 1837-1901) and the style of the same name is still popular now. In the present day we associate the term "Victorian era" with the kind of elegant splendor represented by wedding dresses. However, the term "sophisticated" is also applicable. An "orthodox beauty" is an appropriate description as well.

		3
1		
2		4

1 A Victorian tile ● CD 05_124
This pattern has the image of a satisfying daily life. It has a gentle beauty that blends into the lifestyle.

2 A Victorian tile ● CD 05_125
This continuous design cannot quite be called an arabesque design. The adaptation of a plant shape gives an elegant touch to the design.

3 Book design ● CD 05_126
The originality in this pleasing design conveys a neat and warm atmosphere.

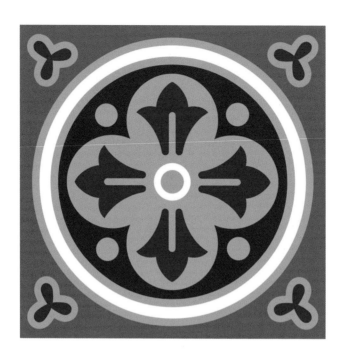

■ Monastery tile (top:twelfth century, bottom:nineteenth century) ● CD 05_127, 128
The flower motif has been adapted to form a design one might associate with knighthood. It conveys an English image with its chic usage of color and retention of a formal touch.

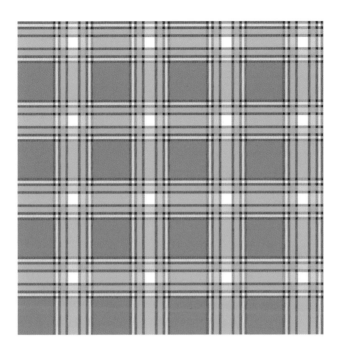

■ **Tartan checks (Scottish patterns) (top: Alberta, bottom: Kincaid)** ● CD 05_129, 130
There are innumerable tartan check patterns. They each have different names such as "Kincaid tartan" or "Bisset tartan" but what is impressive is that they all belong to the same group of "tartan checks."

● CD 05 131 – 133
Switzerland

Swiss wall decorations conveying a bright cheerfulness

The image of Switzerland one most often has is: the platinum mountains in the clear air, an invigorating greenness. The healing beauty of this country can also be seen in the murals on the town buildings that still remain today. The designs convey the joy of life with their brightness, which does not suggest a history of suffering. The designs range from the ancient church paintings from the twelfth century, to the dignified murals displaying the family crest under the eaves of individual homes that can be seen still today.

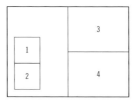

1 **Private house mural** ● CD 05_131
No evidence has been found to show the period when this mural was painted. When the pattern is arranged in parallel lines, the design gives the impression of lovely wrapping paper.

2 **Housing mural** ● CD 05_132
This design was painted as a kind of signboard.

3 **Housing mural** ● CD 05_133
This design was created by changing the combination of parts of patterns, transforming the elements in the design and producing quite a different effect.

◉ CD 05 134 – 136
Holland

Holland is not just windmills—it has a sense of nostalgia that is very Dutch

There is a saying in Holland that suggests the upright character of the Dutch people, "God made the world but the Dutch made Holland." Even now, Holland has various features that make it a trustworthy and elevated culture. It may be due to the deep historical connections that Japan had with Holland that the Dutch patterns from the sixteenth and seventeenth centuries have a kind of nostalgic feel.

		3
1		
2		4

1 Sixteenth-century tile ◉ CD 05_134
When looking at this design it is clear that the Dutch were fond of the Japanese pottery and porcelain patterns.

2 Nineteenth-century cross-stitch ◉ CD 05_135
This folk art floral border pattern conveys a warm spiritual straightforward feel.

3 Mural from the Renaissance period ◉ CD 05_136
Holland was also influenced by the European Renaissance style and this design demonstrates the way it developed in Holland.

⦿ CD 05 137 – 139
Austria

A sense of beauty with a slight touch of individuality

If you link the long history of the rule of the European royal Hapsburg family (1278-1918) and the cultural tone, an atmosphere that is shared with Germany becomes apparent. In the realm of music, Austria enjoys a special rank as the country where Mozart lived. However, even if the patterns are beautiful they do not convey a strong sense of being Austrian.

		3
1		
2		4

1 **An outside window frame decoration**
⦿ CD 05_137
This design was drawn in the Renaissance style. This is a well-constructed design that seems to be based on a honeysuckle pattern, but that is rather unclear.

2 **Decorative design on a hotel building**
⦿ CD 05_138
A fascinating effect is created in this design by the way the motifs of grapes, trees, fountains, and birds are drawn with unique lines.

■ **An outside window frame decoration**
⦿ CD 05_139
Analyzed from a rococo-style viewpoint this appears to be a design drawn in around the eighteenth century. The liveliness of the design is created by the interesting outer edge. Viewed three-dimensionally the wrapped leaves become prominent.

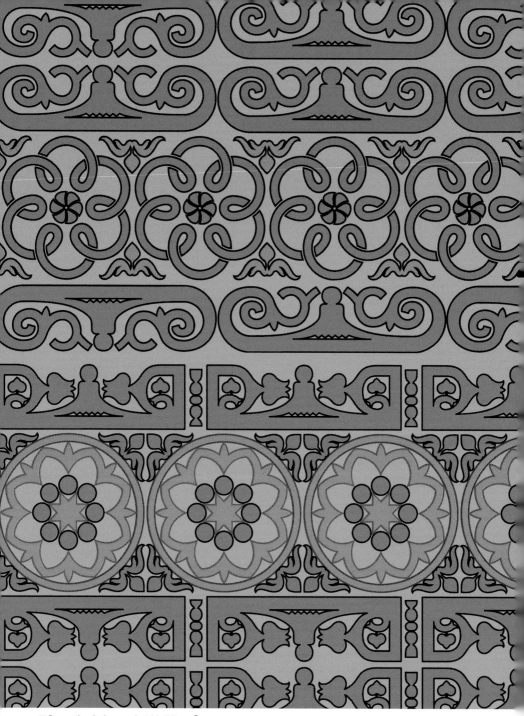

■ **Decorative design on a hotel building** ● **CD 05_140, 141** This design is created from a combination of various patterns. Each part of it is has a solid construction. This design does not have limited usage; it is a design that can support many different kinds of modifications.

■ **An outside window frame decoration** ● **CD 05_142** The style of this design is not limited to a certain style, and it can be used as material to help produce a neat and pretty finish.

■ **Hotel outside window frame decoration** ● **CD 05_143** This is a stately decoration that gives a strong impression of its historical background. The style can be described as baroque.

Chapter 6
Europe – 5
Spain, Portugal, Sweden, Russia, Uzbekistan, Czech Republic, and Belgium

⊙ CD 06 144 – 146
Spain

The immeasurable charm of the other side of a passionate country

"A Passionate country" is a common expression used to describe Spain. In fact, it does give that impression but as the painful expressions on the faces of the flamenco dancers show us, it also has an important, secret other side. A country that produced such talented artists as Picasso and Dali, has an immeasurable charm.

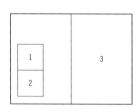

1 Majolica pottery ⊙ CD 06_144
Art nouveau has an aesthetic appeal. A view of the Renaissance style from Majolica reveals a nonconformist, unusual style.

2 A tile from around the seventeenth century
⊙ CD 06_145
This design does not look very Spanish, but it could be described as a design that has many diverse uses.

3 Alhanbura Palace arabesque pattern
⊙ CD 06_146
This is an Islamic design but it has great appeal as an arabesque pattern. The simple composition is spellbinding.

● CD 06 147 – 149
Portugal, Sweden

Accessible patterns of a different dimension

■ Portugal is adjacent to Spain and it has had a range of diverse and conflicting influences on Portugal's history; from the ancient Phoenicians, Carthaginians, and Greeks who moved there, to the Romans who ruled over the land in the era before Christ. Also, it was a country that gave Japan a glimpse of another country outside of Asia. In the same way that Portuguese influenced the Japanese language at one time, the Japanese also feel an affinity toward these attractive designs.

■ Although there may be few patterns produced by northern European countries that are exceptionally interesting from a cultural viewpoint, the traditionally heavy knitwear has an attractive, warm feel to it.

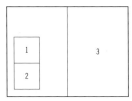

1 2 Two tiles from the eighteenth century
● CD 06_147, 148
These pretty patterns are very likeable. They have the added attraction of lending themselves to adaptations of their designs.

3 Pattern woven in a bulky sweater ● CD 06_149
This pattern gives a rather humorous impression. It is unclear when exactly it was made but the pattern has a handicraft-style appeal that is popular even now.

● CD 06 150 – 152
Russia, Uzbekistan

The non-European feel of the Slavic and Caucasian patterns

Russia is a comparatively young country. It is impossible to describe that vast country in one word but the native Russian culture was strongly influenced by the advanced European countries. However, the Slavic and Caucasian designs have a slightly different, non-European feel to them.

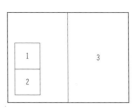

1 Slavic folk tile ● CD 06_150
The design gives a rather heavy and childish impression but there are many such patterns with a warmth that appeals to human nature.

2 A carpet from the Caucasian region ● CD 06_151
The pattern in this carpet is said to express a welcoming greeting to friends who have been invited to the house. It has a rather unfamiliar image.

3 Weaving from Uzbekistan ● CD 06_152
The individual parts of this pattern do not have any particularly special qualities, but we can learn something by looking at the color effect produced by the large number of brightly-colored patterns.

● **CD 06** 153 – 155

Czech Republic, Belgium

Czech ethnic clothing and Belgian art nouveau

■ Before the changes that took place at a bewildering speed in the recent history of the Czech Republic, the country was under the rule of the European Hapsburg family for a long time. So the designs are rather similar to those of Poland, Hungary, Austria, and Switzerland. It's interesting to see the designs that show the local bohemian aesthetic qualities.

■ As Belgium is an area where the art nouveau style developed, the refined designs convey a sense of high culture.

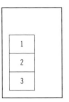

1	
2	
3	

1 2 Two examples of embroidered patterns on ethnic clothing ● CD 06_153, 154

These patterns were used on the borders around the neckline, shoulders, arms, and waist. The neat arrangements in these designs are very familiar even today.

3 nineteenth century Belgian style ● CD 06_155

This design shows a dignified and rather unusual composition of colors. When used in a continuous pattern it gives quite a different effect than in this isolated example. The flower in the pattern is lavender.

Chapter 7

Europe – 6

Art Nouveau, Art Deco

● CD 07 156 – 159
Art Nouveau – 1

A new art style that permeated nearly every aspect of daily life

The new form of art that took the world by storm from 1890 to 1920 had the Eastern perspective of nature as its motif. Under the premise that there are no straight lines in nature, the main constituents of the design were vibrant and flowing curved lines. But it should be added that they were not simply just curved lines, they were of a design that was clearly stylized by the realm of art nouveau. This style of design permeated nearly every aspect of people's lives.

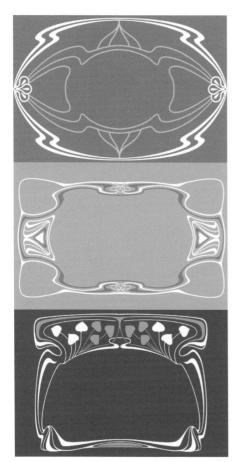

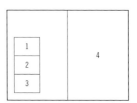

1 2 3 4 Enclosure (frame)
● CD 07_156, 157, 158, 159
These designs are samples used to learn about the style of art created by the representative founder of the art-nouveau style, Alfonse Musha. They were developed by referring to the complicated and skillfully developed masterpiece sketches of Friedrich Adler.

■ Enclosure (frame) ● CD 07_160, 161, 162, 163

● CD 07 164 – 167
Art Nouveau – 2

Concrete representations expressed by the curved lines of art nouveau

The glassware artists Rene Lalique and Emile Galle are well-known. Art nouveau artists introduced various motifs from nature into their work in order to achieve their own independent style of curved lines. Of course that included plants, stems, and flowers, but they also were stimulated to create artistic designs by insects, birds, fish, and running water, anything existing in the natural world that they found inspiring.

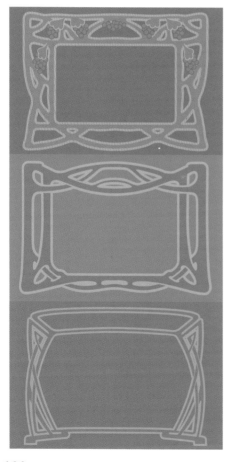

1	4
2	
3	

1 2 3 4 Wooden Frames
● CD 07_164, 165, 166, 167
The vitality of the wood is expressed by these impossible curved lines. As an expression of nature is at the heart of these designs, they convey a feeling of calm.

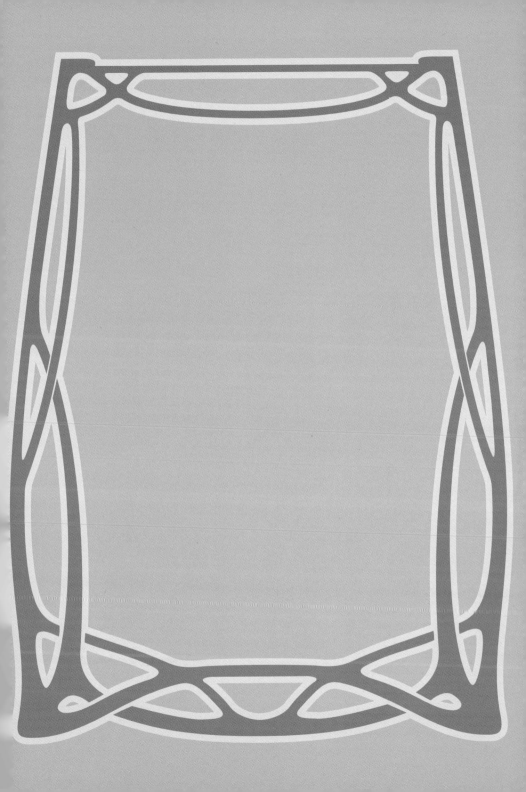

■ **Other frames** ● CD 07_168, 169, 170, 171, 172, 173 It is rather interesting to try using various things in the immediate environment such as string, smoke, and flowers to adapt the design. By choosing the materials you want you can create an excellent work of art.

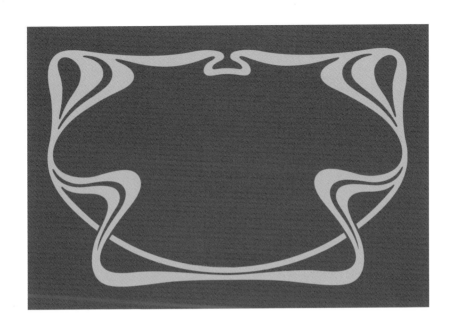

● CD 07 174 – 176

Art Nouveau – 3

The essence of Art Nouveau style is "art for art's sake"

These patterns of flowing curved lines can be used on many different things such as buildings, furniture, and everyday tools. In other words, it has become a kind of fanatical trend. This style, which is also called aestheticism, is a kind of art which dictates a lifestyle with art as the central theme.

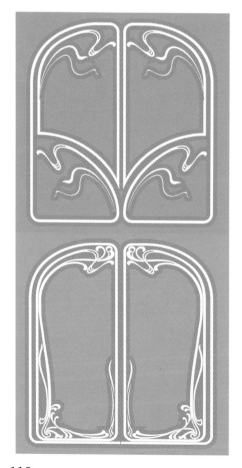

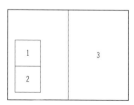

1 2 3 Edging ● CD 07_174, 175, 176
This design was selected from among glass door designs and developed. Although its qualities only seem to be suited to furniture, the strong character of the design has been preserved

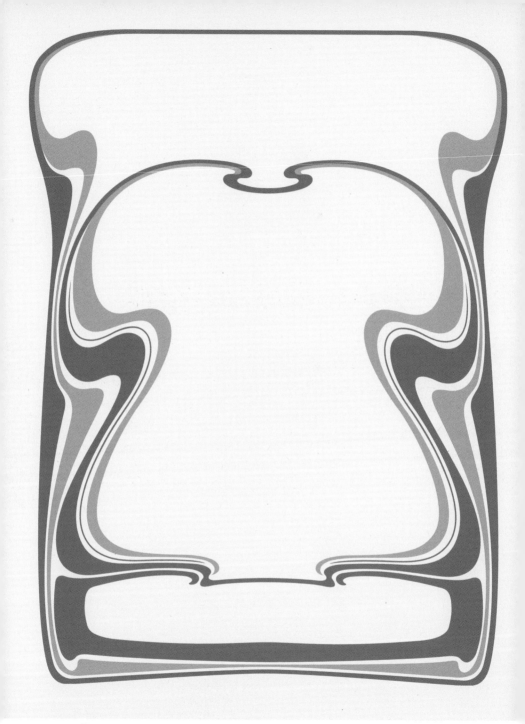

■ **Edging** ● **CD 07_177, 178** Art nouveau posters or promotional notices are created by employing this style.

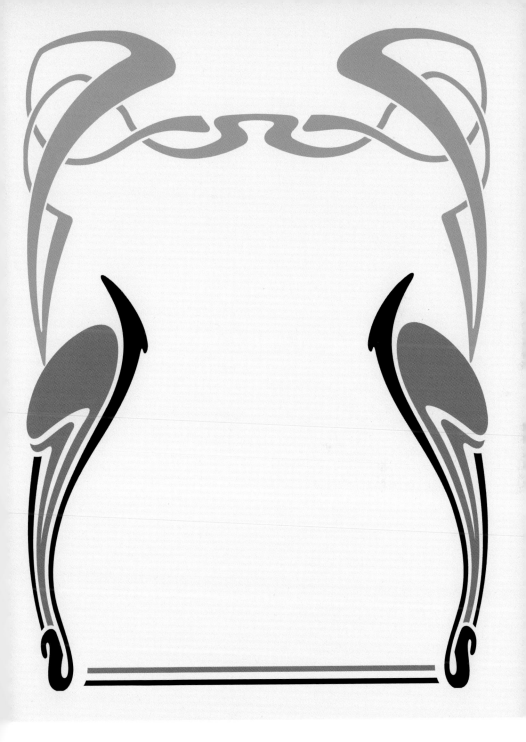

● CD 07 179 – 182

Art Nouveau – 4

The modern way of using the naturally casual beauty of the flowing curved lines

There was one time when the aesthetics of the art nouveau style "art for art's sake" sought to change the style of all art forms. But even now when you walk along the streets or Paris of Brussels surrounded by the flowing lines of art nouveau, there is no feeling of it being out of place. On the other hand, it is impossible to overlook the style and just as you become aware of the actual thought "I'm surrounded by beautiful curved lines" the lines seems to take on a kind of menacing quality.

1		4
2		
3		

1 2 3 4 Symmetry
● CD 07_179, 180, 181, 182
These curved lines look rather like ornaments. There are some difficulties in adapting these designs but by rearranging the lines interesting designs can be created.

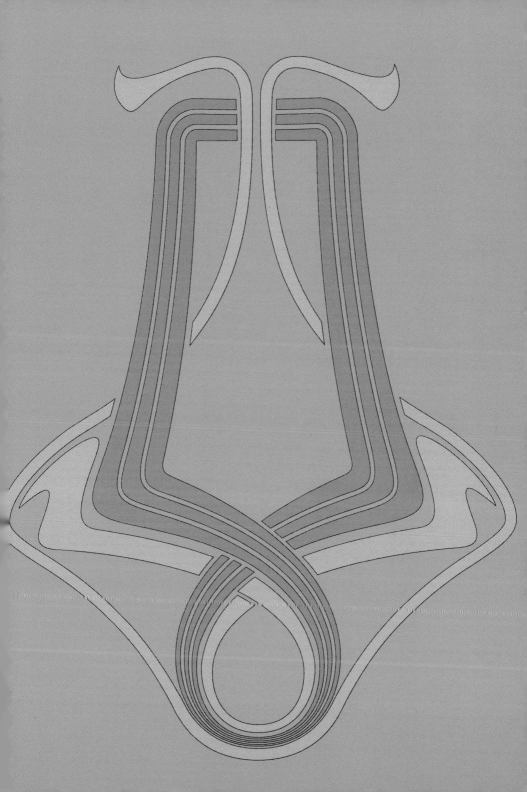

■ **Dyed colors** ● **CD 07_183, 184, 185, 186** By increasing or decreasing the lines and changing the coloring, there is no end to the number of different patterns that can be created.

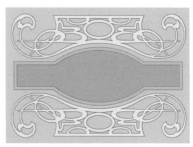

■ **Individual patterns and continuous patterns** ● CD 07_187, 188, 189, 190, 191, 192
At present such a strong effect in a design is not necessary. Here as well, if the pattern is tidied up and the colors carefully selected, it can be developed into interesting patterns that display a fresh softness.

■ **Entrance way doors** ● CD 07_193 This kind of art nouveau doorway fencing can be seen throughout Europe.

● CD 07 194 – 196
Art Deco

Designs that are still living

The quiet trend of art deco has been analyzed as possessing a distinctive beauty that surpasses the limitation of "style." The origin of art deco started in the International Exhibition of Modern Decorative and Industrial Arts held in Paris in 1925 and, as a result of this connection, it is even called the "1925 style." In comparison with the abundant use of curved lines in art nouveau, art deco often employs a streamlined design of geometric straight lines and may be viewed as a counter-movement to art nouveau. However there are many artists who used both styles of art in their work.

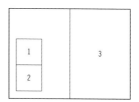

1 2 3 Building Doors (America)
● CD 07_194, 195, 196
The functional beauty of art deco was most widely developed in America. If you look at the whole area of the design it becomes clear that the simple form gives an imposing and dignified effect rather than a decorative splendor.

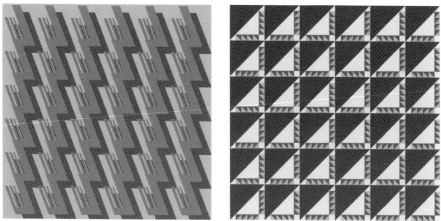

■ **Fabric** ● **CD 07_197, 198** As in example number 196, these patterns also have the special qualities of art deco composition. Of course they also contribute a simplicity that lends itself to adaptation.

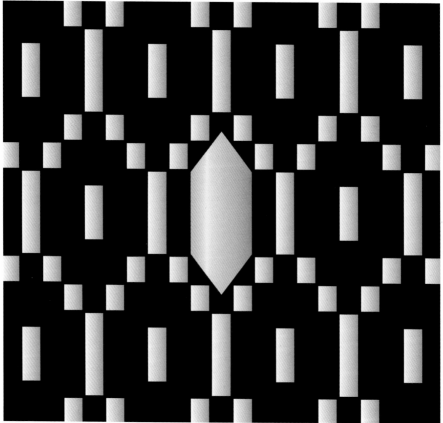

■ **Case for a lid** ● **CD 07_199** The artistic expressions in art deco often give a metallic impression. Again, that adds to the modern feel of the style.

■ **Clock decoration** ● **CD 07_200** The outside lines appear to be of a different genre. But if this pattern is used in an art deco design, the impression of it being out of place will disappear.

■ **Record label** ● **CD 07_201** Although this design cannot be used just as it is, the quality of the configuration can be used well as a reference.

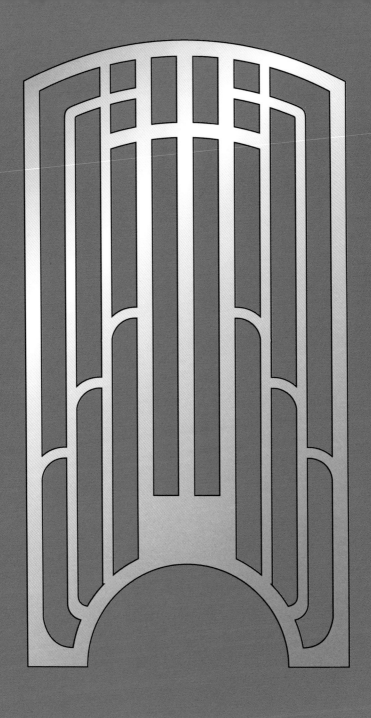

■ **Part of a radio design** ● CD 07_202   The pattern not only conveys the meaning of the design, but also the balance of the vertical and pliable horizontal lines is magnificent.

Chapter 8
The Middle East and Far East

● CD 08 203 – 205
Persia – 1

Patterns from Persia, a country with a strong individuality

Persia is otherwise known as Iran and we are familiar with the Persia of the "Arabian Nights" stories. However, throughout the country there are romantic designs displaying a strong individual image, and they are not just limited to Persian carpets. One is the kilim weave and another is the Islamic pattern. The composition of a kilim woven pattern is made with a sense of the horizontal and vertical lines. Each one of them has a meaning and it is said that they even show the area of origin.

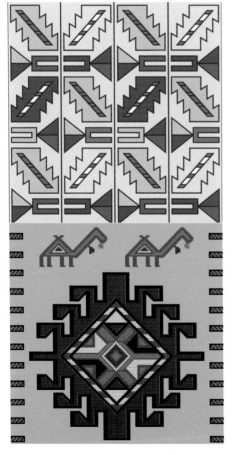

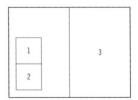

**1 2 Part of a kilim pattern from Guchan
(Northern Iran)** ● CD 08_203, 204
These extracts of patterns were selected for their ability to create an atmosphere. Even among kilim designs, these examples display rather unusual patterns and colors.

3 Design from Iran, mosque decoration
● CD 08_205
This is a beautiful geometric design. However, care must be taken when you are tempted to use this design. The technique of constructing the lines should be learned.

● CD 08 206 – 210
Persia – 2

The inimitable and unique style displayed by Islamic patterns

Original oriental patterns emphasize a bold contrast and a shape that appears mesmerizing. In the early period of Islam, idol worship was banned so this probably also contributed an impetus to the development of a religious style of geometric and floral designs. This is an inimitable and unique style created by an ethnic group that historically made abundant use of these designs in such items as carpets.

	4
1	
2	5
3	

1 Part of a Persian carpet ● CD 08_206
The intermingling of straight and curved lines in this Persian carpet gives a glimpse of a mysterious world. However, by extracting a part of the design in this way, we can see how a simple design is blended in an extremely skillful way.

2 3 Part of a kilim design from Shiraz (Southern Iran) ● CD 08_207, 208
The shapes that jump out at you from this pattern are said to symbolically represent hopes, ideals and wishes.

4 Iranian mosque wall decoration ● CD 08_209
This resembles Arabian lettering but the aim of the design is more to heighten the aesthetic appeal of the pattern.

5 Ancient Islamic tiles ● CD 08_210
These mysterious curvilinear lines create the feel of the world of the "Arabian Nights."

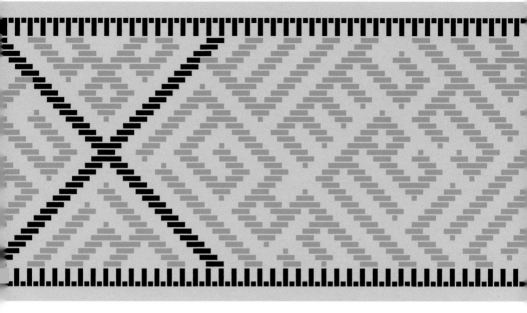

CD 08 211 – 213
Turkey

Original designs using the flower motifs of the Ottoman period

Turkey is a country in which a wide range of cultures coexist, from the cultures of ancient Greece and the Roman Empire to Islamic culture. During the Ottoman period in the sixteenth century there was some imitation of Persian designs and from this background a vast range of designs were created. The designs incorporating flowers, in particular, convey an original atmosphere and there are many designs that achieve a high degree of perfection.

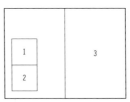

1 Mosque decoration (sixteenth century)
◉ CD 08_211
This example represents a rather unusual form of design in the Islamic world. Such a pattern expresses Turkey's individuality.

2 Part of a kulim from Ushak (Western Turkey)
◉ CD 08_212
This is a border design for a kulim. The pattern in the middle of the design is a popular design often seen in Iranian kulims.

3 Pattern drawn on a glass ball (sixteenth century)
◉ CD 08_213
This is an original Turkish design. There are more intricate compositions with the chrysanthemum as motif but on the whole they all convey this kind of atmosphere.

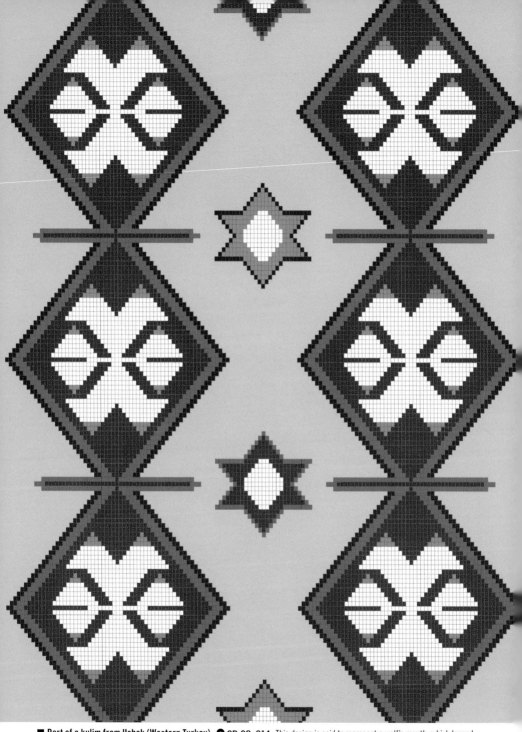

■ **Part of a kulim from Ushak (Western Turkey)** ● CD 08_214 This design is said to represent a wolf's mouth, which legend has it can ward off evil spirits. The surrounding parts often depict motifs of tulips or birds.

Chapter 9
Africa

● CD 09 215 – 218
Africa – 1

Unique design effects clearly conveying the worship of nature

If we closely observe the great lands of Africa it becomes clear that the customs and culture in each area are completely different. Figures and forms from the surrounding natural world that impart meaning to everyday life are freely framed to encourage the worship of nature. The feeling conveyed by such distinctive designs sometimes has the energy to give strength. The Islamic countries of Egypt and Morocco in the Northern area have more of a European sense of aesthetics. Their designs are rich and varied with a sense of softness and there are special meanings in the patterns.

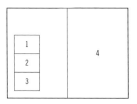

1	4
2	
3	

1 Clay-dyed cloth (West African Belt) ● CD 09_215
The way that all of the animals are facing the same way creates a superb design and depicts lively movment.

2 Clay-dyed cloth (Republic of Mali) ● CD 09_216
This abstract pattern is the most often used design by African Americans. Although it may not have a deep meaning, it is brimming with vitality which can inadvertently create a profoundly impressive effect.

3 4 Dyed cloth from Zimbabwe illustrated with saza (made from corn) ● CD 09_217, 218
The simplicity and strength in these designs are not the result of a conscious effort but are more the result of the pure and natural joy with which the designs were made.

⊙ CD 09 219 – 221
Africa – 2

Patterns showing status and brimming with a sense of luxury

There were many different monarchies in the lands of Africa over which various countries in Europe fought jurisdiction. This is also evident in the traditional designs from these countries. These convincing clay-dyed designs created by the African people are brimming with a sense of luxury. The completely different quality of their clear and detailed patterns seems to be telling us a story about class and status.

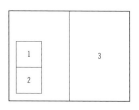

1 **Hand-sewn cloth (West Africa)** ⊙ CD 09_219
This is a mysterious design that gives the feel of a traditional folk tale. It appears to have special usage.

2 **Printed cloth** ⊙ CD 09_220
This design is used by the upper classes of African people. The luxurious finish is created with the help of metallic colors.

3 **Gold-colored cloth** ⊙ CD 09_221
This is a traditional design used by the upper classes. The original design of the pictures printed on the surface creates an excellent design.

● CD 09 222 – 224

Morocco

Geometric patterns influenced by Islam

These designs give more of a strong Islamic, rather than an African, impression because of the geographic location of Morocco and the fact that it is not presently a member of the African Union. There are many Islamic patterns among the Moroccan designs.

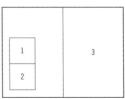

1 2 3 Fez Royal Palace decoration
● CD 09_222, 223, 224

This design represents Islamic geometric patterns. Even if the appeal of the interesting composition of these designs is infinitely developed, the design cannot escape its Islamic influence.

⦿ CD 09 225 – 227
Egypt

A country that still retains its strong individuality from the era before Christ

Egypt was the birthplace of civilization and it experienced the rises and falls in history around 3,000 B.C. At the present time Egypt's own culture is a mosaic-like blend of the cultures from Greece, Rome, and the Islamic world.

1	3
2	

1 2 Hand-sewn cloth pattern ⦿ CD 09_225, 226
There is no clear evidence when these designs originated but they appear to make use of an ancient design. The flowers are drawn in an Egyptian style.

3 Designs on building doors ⦿ CD 09_227
The uniqueness of these designs can be understood when we assume that each design was attached to a different private home.

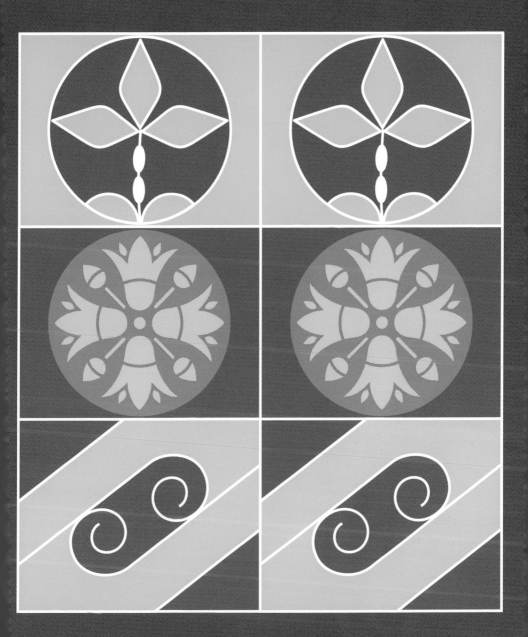

■ **Church decoration from the Byzantine era** ● CD 09_228   This design represents a resting place under the densely growing maple trees. However, the structure also resembles a grapevine.

Chapter 10
The Americas and Oceana

● CD 10 229 – 231

America

A sense of beauty shared by the "Early American" patterns

Excluding the traditional Native American culture, the history of America has not been very long, so what we think of "American" is probably more "Early American." The charm of "Early American" does not only appear to be because they were created by a multi-ethnic country. If we ignore the specific era when these designs were created, they all appear to share a common sense of beauty.

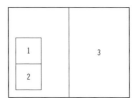

1 2 3 Early American Quilts
● CD 10_229, 230, 231
There are as many American quilts as there are stars but all of them look like they were made by ones grandmother; they have a wholesome appearance and are brimming with tender affection.

■ **Decoration on the metal part of a register** ● CD 10_232, 233, 234 This design was influenced by art nouveau. In the period when the country was growing into a major economic power, America shifted its simple and unsophisticated taste towards a high level of regard for a sense of European aesthetics.

● CD 10 235 – 238

Hawaii

Traditional Hawaiian patterns that respect the formalities of the monarchy

Traditional Hawaii is quite different from the resort feel that it amply projects now. It has a culture that places importance on formalities in a setting of a slowly flowing lifestyle amid breathtaking natural beauty. Pride in the richness of this life is expressed in the style of the traditional patterns that are used in everyday life.

1	4
2	
3	

1 2 3 Hawaiian quilts ● CD 10_235, 236, 237
Rather than having a tropical brightness, these patterns can be described as having a grand and dignified tone.

4 Dyed Clothing ● CD 10_238
When a bright coloring is used, the design undoubtedly becomes tropical, but this blend of colors that is also popular for Japanese tones is, again, definitely Hawaiian.

⊙ CD 10 239 – 242
Oceania

Designs in new countries that reflect the motherland traditions

A relatively large number of traditional designs can be seen in new countries that that do not have their own traditional designs, on islands that have been developed as resorts and even on the islands that have not introduced modern technology. In fact, these designs reflect the traditions of the original home countries of the clients and producers.

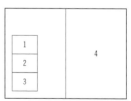

1	4
2	
3	

1 Tile pattern (Santa Katarina) ⊙ CD 10_239
This is in fact a design created by a Spanish artisan in response to an order. However, it is an openhearted design that conveys the mood of the resort of Santa Katarina.

2 Tile pattern (Australia) ⊙ CD 10_240
A design made by using the traditional British argyle (diamond-shaped and colored check) pattern.

3 Tile pattern (Malibu) ⊙ CD 10_241
This is said to have a Californian style.

4 A tile pattern made by using a transfer (nineteenth century) ⊙ CD 10_242
The design has a rococo style and yet is almost too simple. It was created in England during the Victorian era.

◉ CD 10 243 – 245

Peru, Inca

Everyday designs borrowed from the Incas' worship of nature

The symbol of Peru is the high-flying Andes condor. The ethnic cultures of South America endowed the bird with the symbols for freedom and trust and developed designs from this. These geometric designs that have an appeal as textile-or-mosaic style decorations are used for everyday cloth or other objects.

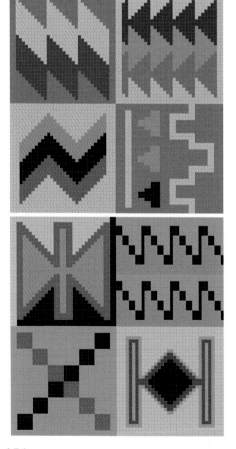

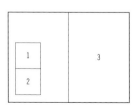

	3
1	
2	

1 2 3 Wool Tapestry ◉ CD 10_243, 244, 245
The color tones of these tapestries convey a relaxed feel, perhaps because they were made from plant dyes. The patterns in these abstract designs may also hold hidden religious meanings characteristic of the relevant ethnic group.

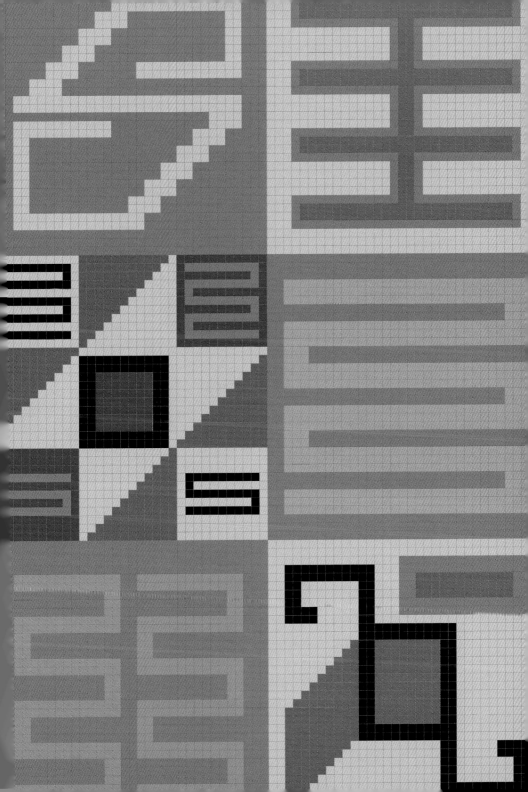

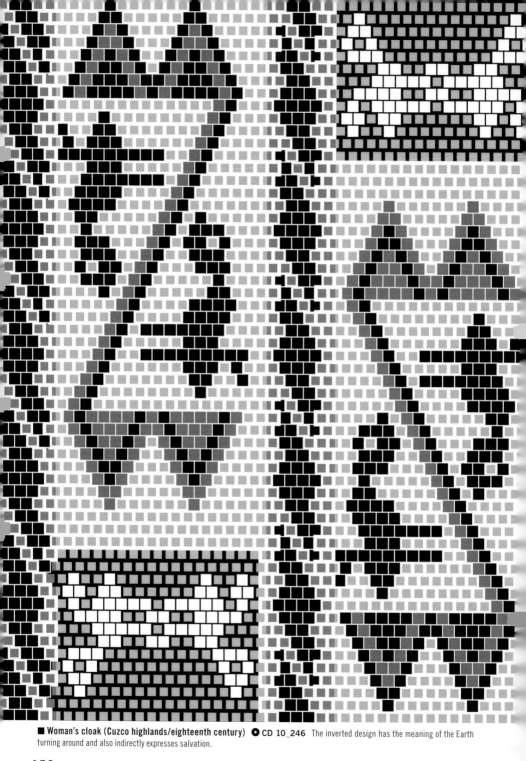

■ **Woman's cloak (Cuzco highlands/eighteenth century)** ● **CD 10_246** The inverted design has the meaning of the Earth turning around and also indirectly expresses salvation.

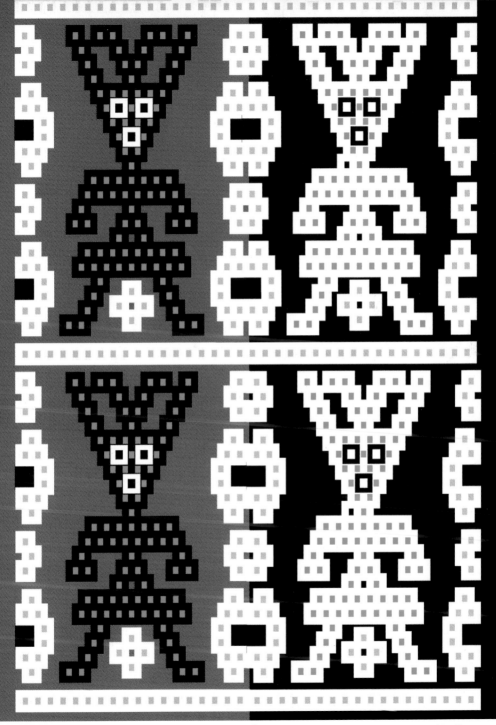

■ **Woman's cloak (Cuzco highlands/eighteenth century)** ● CD 10_247 This pattern is used for ceremonies and is said to depict warriors.

◉ CD 10 248 – 250
Mexico, Maya

The feeling of the bold and colorful Mayan artistic expression rooted in nature worship

The energy bursting from these simple and primitive shapes and the bold expressions rooted in a worship of nature have a special place among the traditional designs from around the world. The combination of the juxtaposing qualities of precise intricacy and wildness in these designs, conveys a kind of human warmth that has a healing effect. This appeal is created by the expression of ethnic tones and magical religious beliefs in the shapes and colors.

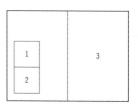

1	3
2	

1 2 3 Part of a clothing design (Guatemala)
◉ CD 10_248, 249, 250
These patterns represent the passage of time. The unlimited bright and colorful tones do not convey the image of the history of persecution that the Mayans suffered. On the contrary, they give the impression of a strong and brave invocation,

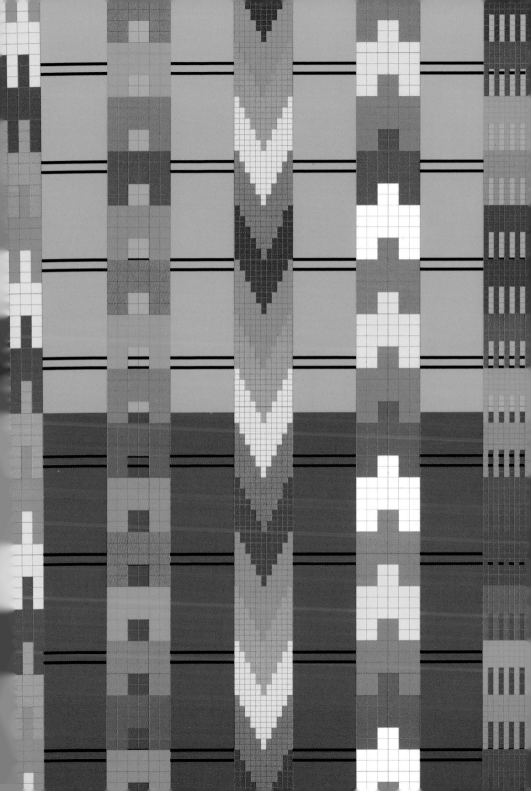

[About the Attached CD-ROM]
The Attached CD-ROM: Using the Material Provided
The purchaser of this book is permitted unrestricted use of the data recorded on the attached CD-ROM, either in its original form or in a modified fashion.

Credit or other such acknowledgment need not be noted in the event of such use. The data provided may also be used overseas, as use is not regionally restricted. Furthermore, copyright fees or secondary user fees are not required to use this material.

Adobe and Adobe Photoshop are either registered trademarks or trademarks of Adobe Systems, Incorporated registered in the United States and/or other countries. Microsoft, Windows, and Windows XP are either registered trademarks or trademarks of Microsoft Corporation registered in the United States and other countries. Apple, Macintosh, Mac and Mac OS are either registered trademarks or trademarks of Apple Computer, Inc. registered in the United States and other countries.

All other brand and product names and registered and unregistered trademarks are the property of their respective owners.

[About the Author]
Shigeki Nakamura An art director since 1964, he established Cobble Corporation Co. Ltd. in 1987. The company published a book of ESP Pattern Library Digital Materials, which can be seen on its website (http://www.cobbleart.com/). He has received many awards, such as the Minister of International Trade and Industry Award, and he is a member of the JAGDA (Japanese Graphic Designer Association).